WITHDRAWN

Let's Knit

Penguin Random House

Senior designer **Hannah Moore**
Project editor **Anne Hildyard**
US editor **Margaret Parrish**
Photographer **Andy Crawford**
Senior producer **Tony Phipps**
Producer **Dragana Puvacic**
Jacket designer **Amy Keast**
Creative technical support **Sonia Charbonnier**
Managing editor **Penny Smith**
Managing art editor **Marianne Markham**
Art director **Jane Bull**
Publisher **Mary Ling**

First American Edition, 2015
Published in the United States by DK Publishing
345 Hudson Street, New York, New York 10014

Copyright © 2015 Dorling Kindersley Limited
A Penguin Random House Company
15 16 17 18 19 10 9 8 7 6 5 4 3 2
002–274528–Sept/2015

A catalog record for this book is available from
the Library of Congress.
ISBN 978-1-4654-3668-9
DK books are available at special discounts when purchased
in bulk for sales promotions, premiums, fund-raising, or
educational use. For details, contact: DK Publishing Special
Markets, 345 Hudson Street, New York, New York 10014
SpecialSales@dk.com

Printed in China.
All images © Dorling Kindersley Limited
For further information see: www.dkimages.com

A WORLD OF IDEAS
SEE ALL THERE IS TO KNOW

www.dk.com

Make pretty knitted pieces.

Contents

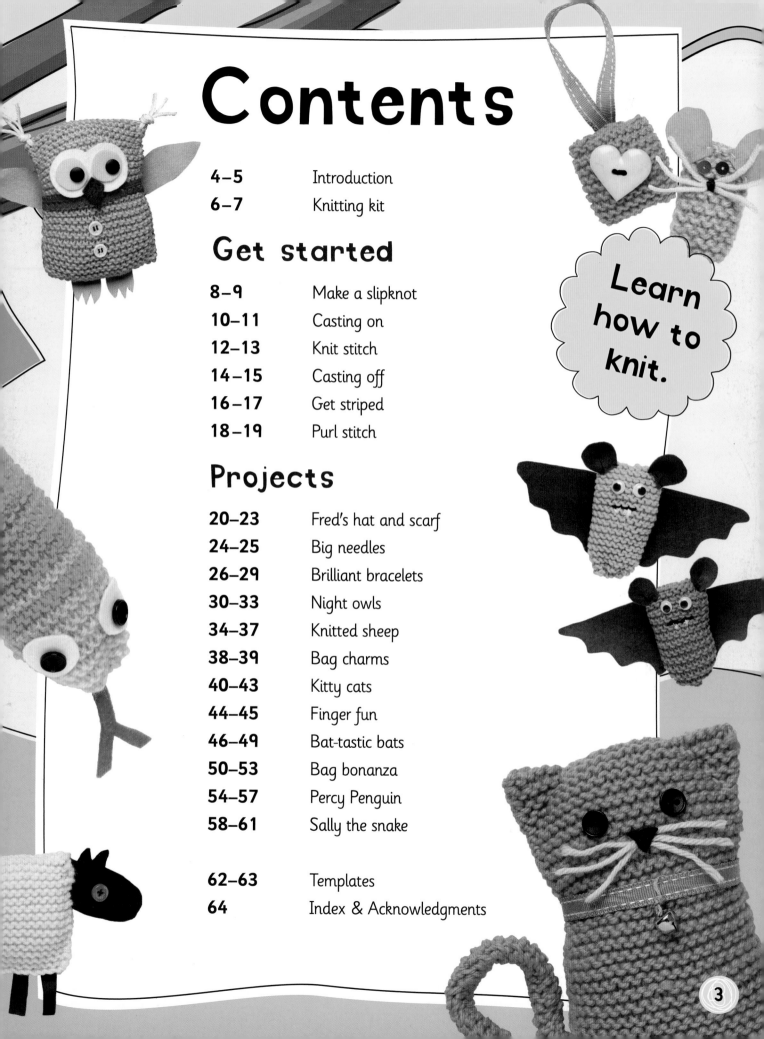

Learn how to knit.

Introduction

To start knitting you need yarn and needles. After that, you can learn how to hold the needles, make a slipknot, cast on, and make a knit and purl stitch. In no time, you'll be knitting. Don't worry about making mistakes—everyone drops stitches at first. With practice, you'll learn to knit well and then you'll be ready to make the adorable projects in this book.

Getting started

At the beginning of each project is a panel listing what **you will need**. With the help of an adult, gather an essential knitting kit (see pages 6–7) and your materials, and start knitting!

Try us! We're really easy to knit.

Safety

All the projects in this book should be made under adult supervision. Always be extra careful when working with knitting needles and when using sharp implements such as scissors, sewing needles, and pins. **Ask an adult to help you.**

Remember to be careful with sharp objects.

Don't be a knitwit! Be safe when you knit.

Knitting kit

Here are the things you need to make all the **projects** in this book.

DK-weight yarn

Knitting needles

Crochet hook

Colored felt

Bet you can't wait to make something!

Chunky yarn

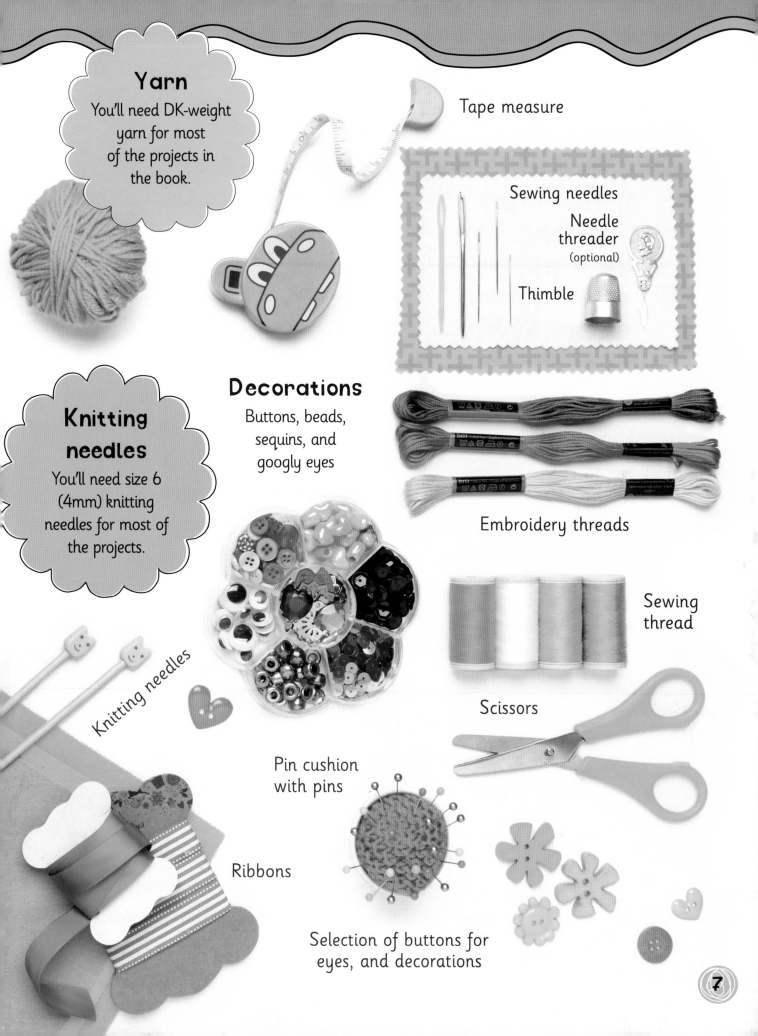

Yarn

You'll need DK-weight yarn for most of the projects in the book.

Tape measure

Sewing needles

Needle threader (optional)

Thimble

Knitting needles

You'll need size 6 (4mm) knitting needles for most of the projects.

Decorations

Buttons, beads, sequins, and googly eyes

Embroidery threads

Sewing thread

Knitting needles

Scissors

Pin cushion with pins

Ribbons

Selection of buttons for eyes, and decorations

Make a slipknot

To start knitting, first you need yarn and needles.
The next step is to make a **slipknot.**

You may get **tangled up** at first...

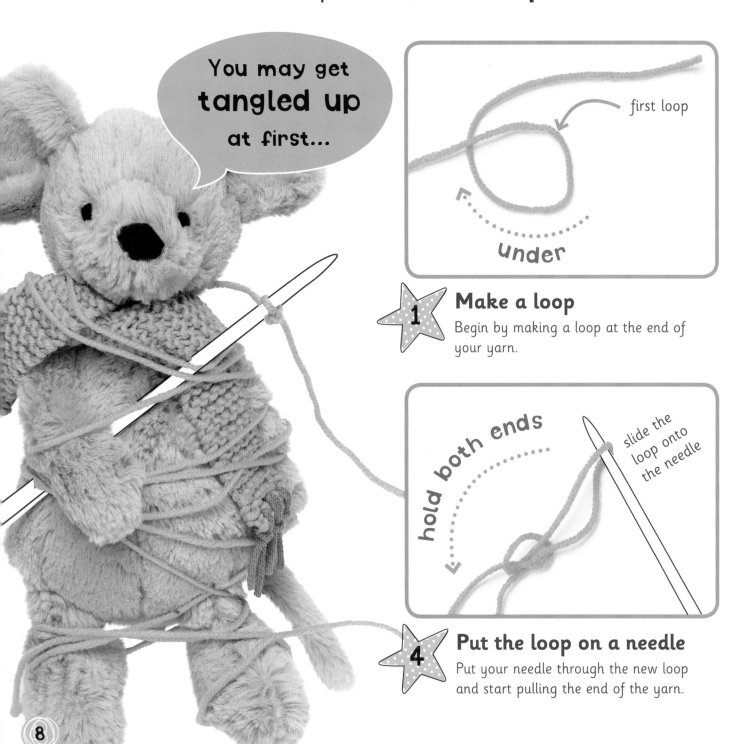

first loop

under

⭐ **1** **Make a loop**
Begin by making a loop at the end of your yarn.

hold both ends

slide the loop onto the needle

⭐ **4** **Put the loop on a needle**
Put your needle through the new loop and start pulling the end of the yarn.

This will become your **first** **stitch**

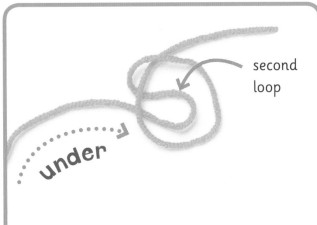

second loop

under

2

Make a new loop
Bring the yarn through the first loop to make a new loop.

pull through

3

Pull the new loop through
Keep pulling the new loop until it is big enough for your needle to go through.

pull tight

... but with practice, you'll be able to make **a perfect slipknot!**

5

Pull the end tight
Keep pulling the yarn until the loop is tight enough to stay on the needle.

Casting on

You've already made your first stitch with your slipknot. Now add as many stitches as you like—then you can begin knitting.

hold the yarn in your **left hand**

make a **loop** on your thumb

1 **Slipknot on the needle**
Before you add any stitches, start with a slipknot on your needle. It's knotted so that it stays on the needle.

2 **Wrap yarn around thumb**
To start making a new stitch, hold the needle in one hand, then wrap the yarn around the front of the thumb.

Now you're **ready** to **start**

Count your stitches **one, two, three...**

1 2 3 4 5 6

hold yarn **tightly**

now you have cast on **two stitches**

3 **Slip needle into the loop**
Put your needle through the loop on your thumb. Gently lift the yarn off your thumb so the loop slips onto the needle.

4 **Pull the yarn tight**
Pull the yarn tight so the loop sits next to the first one you made with the slipknot. Keep going until you have all the stitches you need.

knitting!

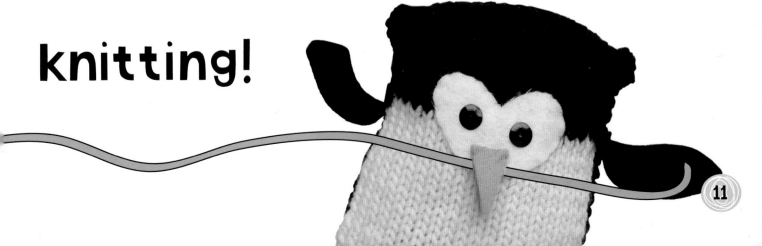

Knit stitch

Percy Penguin has knitted a few rows to get you started. Knit stitch is used in all the projects, and it's easy to learn.

into the loop

wind the yarn firmly around your fingers

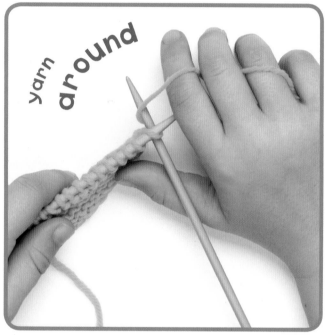

yarn around

1

Start with the first stitch
Push the end of the needle into the front of the first stitch.

2

Wrap yarn around needle
Bring the yarn under and around the needle so the yarn is between the two needles.

When you finish a row, swap the needles

All the stitches are on your **right needle.**

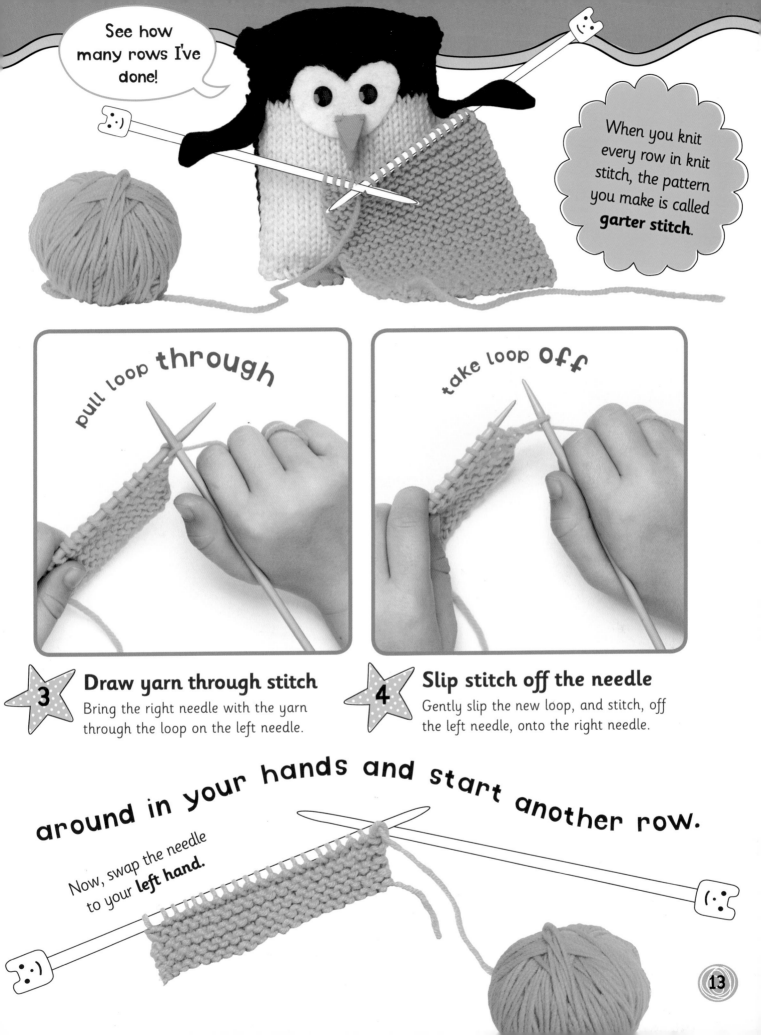

See how many rows I've done!

When you knit every row in knit stitch, the pattern you make is called **garter stitch**.

pull loop **through**

take loop **off**

3 **Draw yarn through stitch**
Bring the right needle with the yarn through the loop on the left needle.

4 **Slip stitch off the needle**
Gently slip the new loop, and stitch, off the left needle, onto the right needle.

around in your hands and start another row.

Now, swap the needle to your **left hand.**

Casting off

When your knitting is the length you want it, it's time to **cast off**. This means leaving a neat edge.

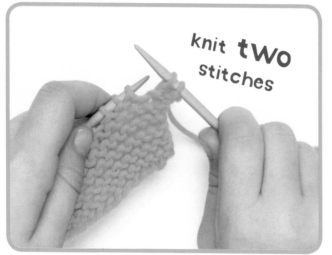

knit **two** stitches

pick up the first **stitch**

 1 **Knit two stitches**
Knit the first two stitches from the left needle onto the right needle.

 2 **Pick up the first stitch**
Push the left needle into the first stitch on the right needle and pick it up.

drop **off**

make a **loop**

 4 **Drop the first stitch**
Let the first stitch drop off the needle. Knit another stitch, then repeat steps 2–4.

 5 **At the last stitch**
With your needle, open out the last stitch to make a big loop.

Sew in the ends

Thread the loose yarn onto a needle and sew down the edge of the knitting.

Pull the needle and yarn through.

Cut the yarn close to the knitting.

The neatened edge looks like this.

lift the stitch **over**

3 Lift the first stitch over

Carefully carry the first stitch over the second stitch.

Cut the yarn and put the end through the loop.

6 Pull yarn through loop

Push the end of the yarn all the way through, and pull tight.

Now that you've learned to knit, why not make a cool scarf like mine?

15

Get striped

Stripes are fun. You can use lots of pretty colors and make thin or fat **stripes,** or a mixture of both.

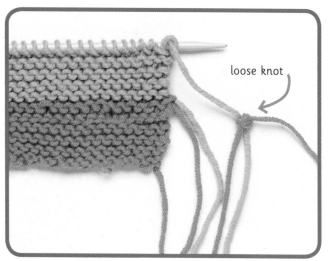

loose knot

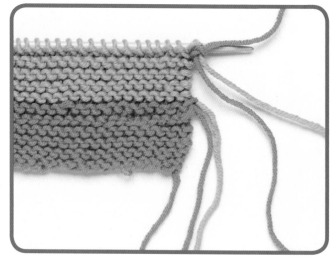

 Joining a new color
Tie the new yarn to the first one with a loose knot.

 Slide the knot up
Carefully move the knot upward until it reaches the needle.

To create even stripes, join a new color at the start of a row.

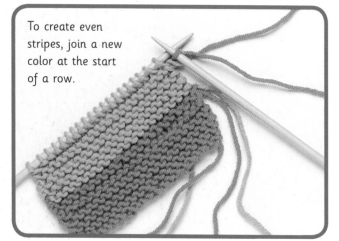

 Start knitting
Now start knitting with the new color.

 Knit to end of the row
Knit as many rows as you like to make a stripe with your new color.

Or try **variegated.**

My stripes were made with variegated yarn.

Easy stripes

It's quicker to use variegated yarns. Since they are made with so many colors, the stripes are created as you knit!

Add color with stunning stripes.

My stripes were made with different colored yarns.

Variegated yarn comes in lots of **color combinations.**

These bags show two different kinds of stripes.

Purl stitch

This is another stitch to learn. Although you do it differently than knit stitch, it looks just the same!

yarn to the **front**

yarn **around** needle

1 **Put the needle in the stitch**
Push the needle into the first stitch. The needle crosses in front of the left needle.

2 **Wrap yarn around needle**
Holding yarn tightly, wrap it around the right needle from right to left.

Knit stitch is at the front.

The front is smooth, with V-shaped stitches.

18

If you knit a row in knit stitch and the next row in purl, you make **stockinette stitch.**

pull needle backward

take off needle

 Pull the needle through
Pull the right needle back and through, taking yarn with it as your new loop.

 Slip loop off left needle
Let the old loop slip off; your new loop will now be on your right needle.

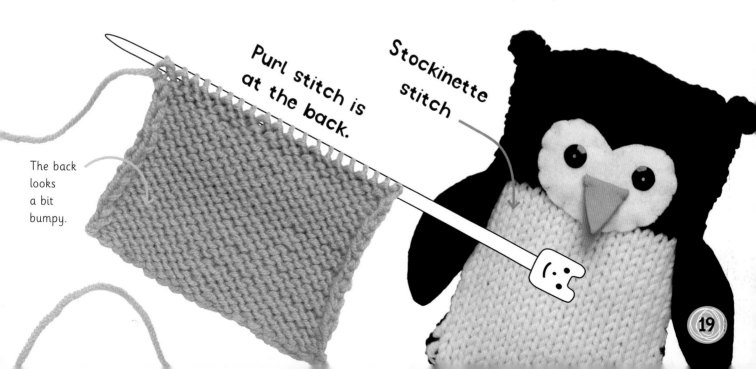

Purl stitch is at the back.

Stockinette stitch

The back looks a bit bumpy.

You will need

DK-weight yarn • pair of size 6
(4mm) knitting needles
• tapestry needle • crochet hook
• scissors • plastic fork

Fred's hat and scarf

This snuggly hat and scarf are finished with a fluffy pom-pom and tassels.

Cast on 20 stitches

Cast on 8 stitches

Fred's hat

Fred's scarf

1 Knit the hat shape

Cast on 20 stitches. Keep knitting until the strip is 8in (20cm) long. Sew in the ends after casting off.

2 Knit the scarf shape

Cast on 8 stitches. Keep knitting until the scarf measures about 11in (28cm) long. Sew in the ends after casting off.

For an extra-long scarf, just keep knitting!

How to finish the hat

Sew a running stitch around one of the open edges.

 Sew up one side
Fold the hat rectangle in half, then pin and sew up one side. Leave the two opposite sides open.

2 **Close up the top**
Pull the yarn tight to close up the top of your hat and secure with one or two stitches.

How to make the scarf tassels

Use a crochet hook.

1 **Cut short pieces** of yarn and hook a loop through the end of the scarf.

2 **Pull the loop** all the way through with the crochet hook.

3 **Thread the ends** of the yarn through the loop. Pull tight and trim with scissors.

How to make a mini pom-pom

1 **Wind the yarn** around a fork and tie a knot in the ends.

wrap around

thread through

2 **Wrap the yarn** around and around. Thread the end through the prongs.

3 **Tie the two ends** of yarn together in a knot.

4 **With scissors,** snip the yarn at each side. Fluff up your pom-pom.

Sew a pom-pom onto the gathered end of the hat.

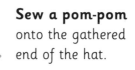

You can also sew on bells or felt shapes to our hats.

If you want to make a **smaller hat**, cast on 15 stitches and knit until the strip is 6in (15cm) long. For a **smaller scarf**, just cast on 6 stitches and knit as many rows as you like.

Big needles

If you like Fred's scarf and want one the same, just "big up" with fatter needles and chunky yarn.

Make yourself a scarf just like mine.

Knit the scarf

Cast on 12 stitches and knit until the scarf is 36in (90cm) long, or as long as you like. Cast off, then sew in any yarn ends.

See how much smaller the knitting is on Fred's scarf.

You will need

chunky yarn • pair of size 17 (12mm) needles • tapestry needle • scissors • crochet hook

If you use thin yarn and fat needles, you'll get loose, lacy knitting.

For fun, make **tassels in a different color** than your scarf. Use as many colors as you like.

Make tassels in the same way as you did for Fred's scarf on page 22.

25

Brilliant bracelets

It's easy to knit these beautiful bracelets, and you can have fun decorating them with sparkly beads, pretty buttons, and ribbons.

Flat bracelets are the quickest and easiest to make. You can knit and decorate them in no time at all.

Rolled up bracelets

Sew your most beautiful **button** to the center of the bracelet.

You will need

DK-weight yarn • pair of size 6 (4mm) knitting needles • tapestry needle • sewing needle • thread • scissors • buttons • beads • ribbons

Flat bracelets

Go crazy!
Show off your creative work by wearing a few bracelets at a time, like here. You'll get lots of orders from your friends!

Striped bracelets

Making **striped** bracelets is a great way to use up leftover yarn.

How to make a rolled bracelet

Cast on 6 stitches

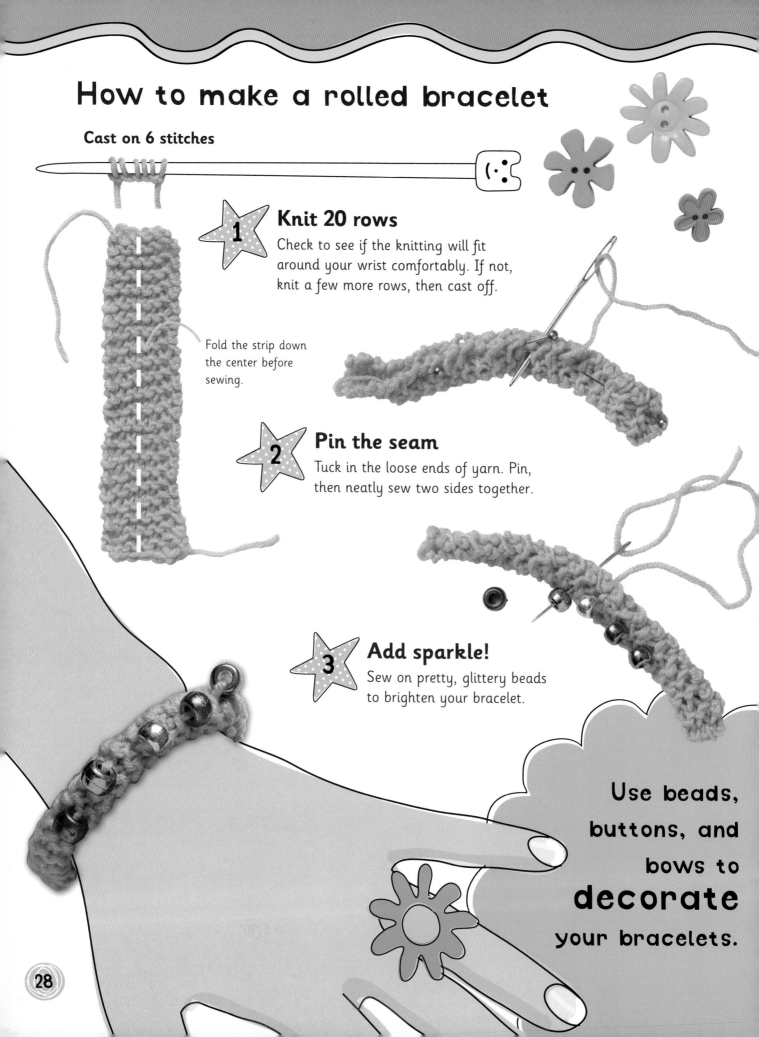

⭐ **1** **Knit 20 rows**
Check to see if the knitting will fit around your wrist comfortably. If not, knit a few more rows, then cast off.

Fold the strip down the center before sewing.

⭐ **2** **Pin the seam**
Tuck in the loose ends of yarn. Pin, then neatly sew two sides together.

⭐ **3** **Add sparkle!**
Sew on pretty, glittery beads to brighten your bracelet.

Use beads, buttons, and bows to **decorate** your bracelets.

Different fastenings

Top tip

You can personalize bracelets to give as gifts by sewing your friends' names on them.

Ribbon fastening

Cut two short lengths of fine ribbon. Sew a length to each end of your bracelet.

Sew the ribbon firmly in place.

Use a loose end of yarn to **sew** the bracelet together.

Circle fastening

Sew the two ends of the bracelet together.

Button and loop fastening

Sew a button to one end of your bracelet. At the other end, pull through a short length of yarn. Make a knot so a loop is formed. Check that it's big enough for your button to fit through.

At one end, sew on a **button**.

Tie a **knot** in the ends of the yarn to make a loop.

29

Whoo wants to learn to knit?

Make a **striped owl** friend in any color—see page 16 to learn how to knit stripes.

You will need

DK-weight yarn • pair of size 6 (4mm) knitting needles • scissors • felt • tapestry needle • polyfill • needle and thread • buttons

Night owls

These owls are a hoot! You can make them one color or striped, and add felt faces and cute little scarves.

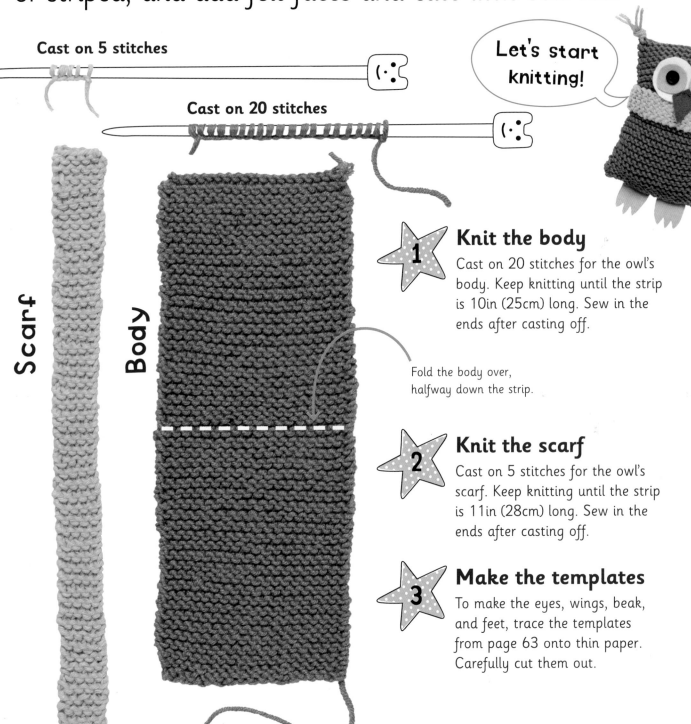

Cast on 5 stitches

Cast on 20 stitches

Let's start knitting!

Scarf

Body

★1 Knit the body
Cast on 20 stitches for the owl's body. Keep knitting until the strip is 10in (25cm) long. Sew in the ends after casting off.

Fold the body over, halfway down the strip.

★2 Knit the scarf
Cast on 5 stitches for the owl's scarf. Keep knitting until the strip is 11in (28cm) long. Sew in the ends after casting off.

★3 Make the templates
To make the eyes, wings, beak, and feet, trace the templates from page 63 onto thin paper. Carefully cut them out.

Make me in one of your favorite colors.

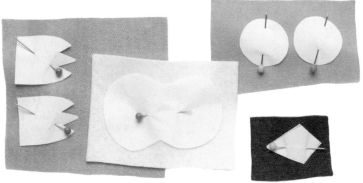

4 **Cut out the felt pieces**
Pin the paper templates onto pieces of felt and carefully cut out the shapes.

5 **Sew up the body**
Using the same yarn that you used for the body, neatly sew around two edges. Then sew halfway along the third side.

Sew the scarf here.

8 **Add the scarf**
Put the scarf around your owl's neck. Pin it together, and then sew to hold it firmly in place.

9 **Attach feet**
Pin the feet to the back of your owl. Sew in place.

Sew on the eyes and beak before you sew them onto the body.

6 Add the filling
Use polyfill to stuff the body, pushing it into the corners. Then sew up the body to hold in the filling.

7 Sew on the face
Sew through the buttons to attach the face to the body.

10 Make tufted ears
Thread a tapestry needle with a short length of yarn. Push it through a top corner of the body. Snip the yarn to release the needle. Tie in a knot and trim. Repeat for the other ear.

Trim my tufted ears to any length you like.

You will need

DK-weight yarn · pair of size 6 (4mm) knitting needles · tapestry needle · thin paper · felt · buttons · needle and thread · polyfill

Baa Baa, white sheep, you are made of wool...

Baa! I love ewe, Mommy.

34

Knitted sheep

Once you get the hang of it, you can knit a whole flock of sheep. If you count them, make sure you don't fall asleep!

Cast on 25 stitches.

★ 1 Knit the body

Cast on 25 stitches. Keep knitting until the strip is 6in (15cm) long. Sew in the ends after casting off.

★ 2 Make the templates

Trace the templates from page 63 onto thin paper. Carefully cut them out.

Fold the body over, halfway down the strip.

Mommy sheep

Top tip
To make extra-soft sheep, use fluffy white wool yarn.

Love you, too.

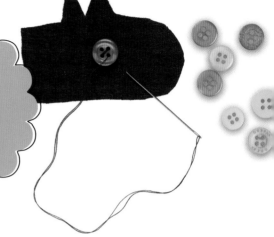

Top tip

For the eyes, find buttons in lots of colors, so your sheep all look different.

⭐ **3** **Cut out the felt**

Pin your paper templates onto felt and carefully cut out the head and legs.

 4 **Sew on the eyes**

For the eyes, sew a button to the middle of each side of the head.

Put the filling in the open head-end of the sheep.

⭐ **7** **Add the stuffing**

Use polyfill to stuff the body. Push it into the corners with a pencil or your finger.

 8 **Sew the head in place**

Put the head in place, pin, and then sew the edges together.

ewe, ram, and lamb.

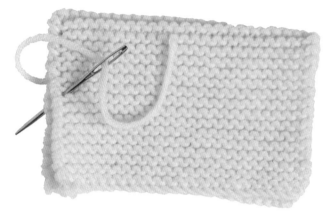

5 Sew up the body
Fold the sheep rectangle in half and sew along one short side.

6 Attach the legs
Pin the legs inside the long, open side, then sew the edges together.

How are you, Woolly?

Not too baaad!

Make a ram
Cast on 25 stitches. Knit a 7in (18cm) strip. Then make in the same way as a mommy sheep.

Find the template for the horns on page 63.

Make a lamb
Cast on 15 stitches. Knit a 4in (10cm) strip. Make the lamb in the same way as the mommy sheep.

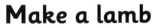

Sew funny faces on **your charms** or decorate them with beads or buttons.

Add tufted ears to this owl charm.

Aren't I charming?

What big eyes I've got!

Bag charms

These cute little charms are perfect for customizing your bags. They make great party bag gifts, too.

You will need

DK-weight yarn • pair of size 6 (4mm) knitting needles • tapestry needle • needle and thread • felt • buttons • polyfill • ribbon

How to make a square charm

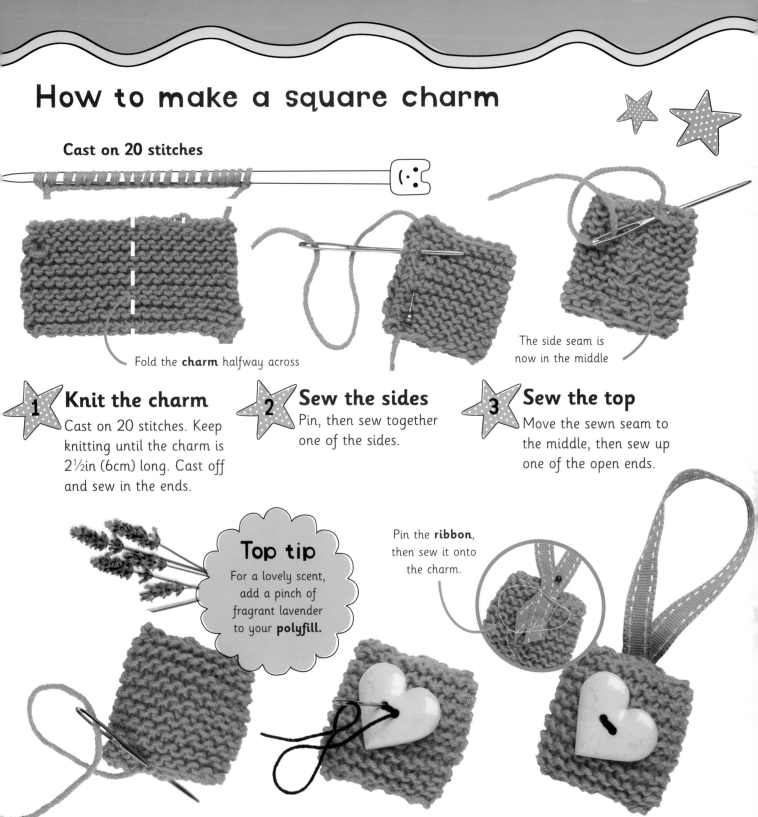

Cast on 20 stitches

Fold the **charm** halfway across

The side seam is now in the middle

1 Knit the charm
Cast on 20 stitches. Keep knitting until the charm is 2½in (6cm) long. Cast off and sew in the ends.

2 Sew the sides
Pin, then sew together one of the sides.

3 Sew the top
Move the sewn seam to the middle, then sew up one of the open ends.

Top tip
For a lovely scent, add a pinch of fragrant lavender to your **polyfill**.

Pin the **ribbon**, then sew it onto the charm.

4 Fill and sew
Push in polyfill, then sew up the last open end to hold in the filling.

5 Add a button
Decorate the charm by sewing on a button.

6 Make a loop
Pin the ends of a ribbon to the back of the charm and sew it in place.

Knitting looks like fun.

Yes, I'd like to learn purr...l. Miaow !

You will need

DK-weight yarn • pair of size 6 (4mm) knitting needles • tapestry needle • polyfill • pencil • needle and thread • buttons • ribbon • bells

To make **a little friend** for your kitten, cast on 10 stitches. Knit 4in (10cm) then proceed as for the larger cat.

Kitty cats

These cool cats are purr...fect. With their stylish collars
and bells, they're the cat's whiskers!

Cast on 18 stitches

Let's get knitting!

Cast on 8 stitches

kitten's body

Fold the
body over
halfway
down.

kitten's tail

Knit the body

Cast on 18 stitches. Keep
knitting until your knitting
is 13in (33cm) long. Cast
off, then sew in the ends.

Knit the tail

Cast on 8 stitches. Knit
until the tail measures 8in
(20cm). Cast off, then sew
in the ends.

Fold the tail
lengthwise down
the center.

You can make us in **any color**... even blue or green!

3 **Sew the two sides**

Pin and sew two sides together. Then sew halfway up the third side, leaving a space to add the filling.

4 **Add the filling**

Use polyfill to stuff the body—push it into the corners with a pencil. Then sew up the opening.

Attach the **whiskers** to the nose first.

Top tip

For a curly tail, put a pipecleaner in the tail before sewing it closed.

7 **Sew on nose and whiskers**

Sew on kitty cat's nose and whiskers, just below the eyes.

8 **Make the tail**

Sew the edges of the tail together. Sew the tail onto the back of the kitten.

Top tip

Instead of buttons, you can glue beads or sequins onto your kitten.

5 Make the ears

Pin and sew across each corner of the head to make the ears.

6 Sew on the eyes

Sew on little buttons to make the eyes.

Pin the kitten's collar at the back before sewing it.

With this bell, I can't sneak up on anyone!

9 Add the collar

Push a piece of thread through a bell and tie it onto the collar. Wrap the collar around the kitten and sew it firmly in place.

Finger fun

Why not put on a show with these funny puppets? They're so quick to knit, you can make one for every finger!

Sew on yarn to make the hair.

Decorate your puppets with sequins, beads, buttons, and scraps of felt, yarn, or fabric.

Attach the felt eyes, sequins, and mouth with fabric glue.

You will need

DK-weight yarn • pair of size 6 (4mm) knitting needles • tapestry needle • needle and thread • felt • buttons • sequins

How to make a finger puppet

Cast on 15 stitches

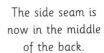

Fold the **charm** halfway across

The side seam is now in the middle of the back.

⭐1 Knit the body

Cast on 20 stitches. Keep knitting until the body is 2½in (6cm) long. Cast off and sew in the ends.

⭐2 Sew the sides

Pin, then sew up one of the sides.

⭐3 Sew the top

Move the sewn seam to the middle, then sew one of the open ends closed.

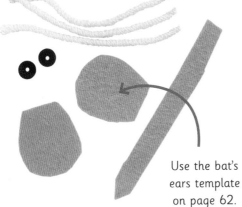

Use the bat's ears template on page 62.

Top tip

If you want bigger **finger puppets**, just use larger knitting needles.

⭐4 Make the extras

Cut out a tail and ears from felt, using the template for the bat's ears. Cut three short lengths of yarn for the whiskers.

⭐5 Sew on the whiskers

Use black thread to sew on the whiskers, so the thread looks like a nose.

⭐6 Sew on the eyes and ears

Sew on sequins for the eyes, and sew the ears and tail to the body.

Want to go out flying tonight?

Bat-tastic bats

With their cute fangs and googly eyes, these batty bats are fun to make. Hang a few up together for a great bat-mobile.

You will need

DK-weight yarn • pair of size 6 (4mm) knitting needles • tapestry needle • thin paper • felt • needle and thread • googly eyes • fabric glue • polyfill

family of lovable little acro-bats!

No, we just want to hang around.

Cast on 22 stitches

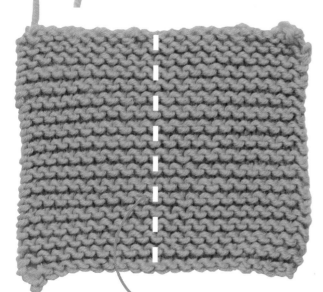

Fold the body down the center.

1 Knit the bat's body

Cast on 22 stitches. Keep knitting until the strip is 3½in (9cm) long. Cast off, then sew in the ends.

2 Make the templates

Trace the templates for the wings and ears on page 62 onto thin paper. Carefully cut them out.

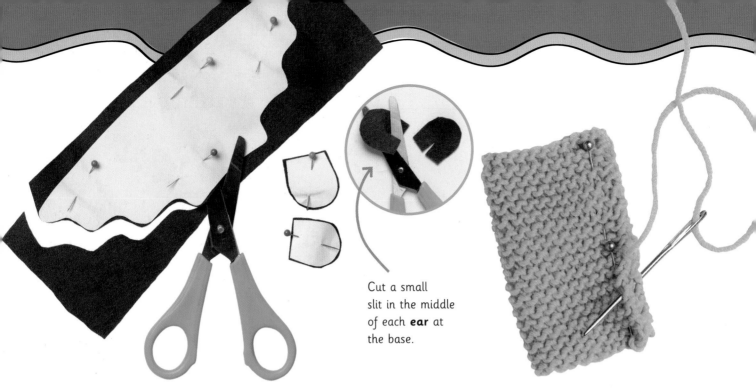

Cut a small slit in the middle of each **ear** at the base.

Cut out the felt pieces

Pin the paper templates onto pieces of felt and carefully cut out the shapes.

Sew the body

Pin the long sides, then neatly sew them together.

3

4

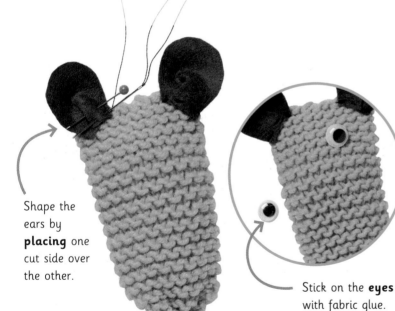

Shape the ears by **placing** one cut side over the other.

Stick on the **eyes** with fabric glue. Press down firmly.

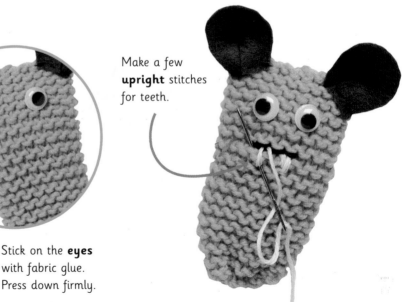

Make a few **upright** stitches for teeth.

7

Sew on the ears

Pin the ears to each side at the top of the body, then sew them on.

8

Add the mouth and teeth

Sew stitches in black thread for the mouth. Use white thread to sew on the fangs.

Move the sewn edges to the center at the back of the bat's body.

Pull tight!

⭐ 5 Add the filling
Pin and sew one of the short sides together. Stuff with polyfill, pushing it into the corners.

⭐ 6 Close up
Sew running stitch along the open end. Pull the thread tight and secure with a stitch.

Let's get a bite to eat!

⭐ 9 Attach the wings
Pin the wings to the center of the bat's back. Sew onto the bat with running stitch.

Top tip
Sew thread to your bat's head so you can hang it up.

knitted straps

bags with long straps

short handles

Knitted handles

Make the handles of your bags **thick or thin**, and knit them as **long or short** as you want. Ribbon handles work too.

Stripes

To learn how to make **stripes**, see pages 15 and 16.

Bag bonanza

Not only do these bags look amazing, but they are also **easy** to make. You can decorate them any way you like.

Pretty!
Rows of braid and ribbons and buttons of different shapes and sizes will make your bags look fabulous.

bags with ribbon straps

bags with sparkly sequins

Decorate with buttons, pom-poms, ribbon, and sequins.

You will need

DK-weight yarn · pair of size 6 (4mm) knitting needles · tapestry needle · needle and thread · ribbon · sequin ribbon · button

Fold the knitting over halfway down the strip.

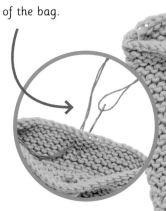

Cast on 25 stitches

1 Knit the bag

Cast on 25 stitches. Keep knitting until the strip is 9in (22cm) long. Cast off, then sew in the ends.

Make a **loop** on the back of the bag.

3 Sew on a button

On the front of the bag, sew on a button. Trim the ends of the thread neatly.

4 Make a button loop

Using a double thickness of thread, sew a loop. Knot the ends together to hold it in place.

More brilliant bag ideas...

Drawstring bag

Make a bag as shown, then thread ribbon or cord about 1in (2.5cm) from the top. Tie a knot in the ends. Pull the ribbon tight to close the bag.

Add a beautiful button that matches the **drawstring**.

⭐ 2 Sew up two sides

Pin the sides, then neatly sew them together.

Sew the ends of the ribbon **handle** to the inside of the bag.

Sew rows of **sequin ribbon** around the bag using running stitch.

Useful pouch

This pouch can be used for a phone, for pencils, or even as a sleeping bag for your small soft toys. Cast on 15 stitches, then knit a strip 12in (30cm) long. Cast off, then sew in the ends. Leave a flap at the top, then sew up the sides.

⭐ 5 Add finishing touches!

Sew ribbon all around the bag to add flair. Next, sew on a length of ribbon to create the handle.

Decorate this cool cell phone case with a **funny face**. Add felt for teeth and buttons for eyes.

You will need

DK-weight yarn • pair of size 6 (4mm) knitting needles • felt • tapestry needle • thin paper • polyfill • needle and thread • fabric glue • sequins

Top tip
For the fish, cut out fish shapes in felt, then sew or glue on a bead for each eye.

Gone fishing! What a catch!

Percy Penguin

You'll need two colors of yarn to make this sweet little penguin. He's so cool!

Cast on 18 stitches in black.

1 Knit the body
Cast on 18 stitches in black yarn. Keep knitting until your knitting is 8in (20cm) long. Change to white yarn and knit 3½in (9cm) in stockinette stitch (alternate rows of knit and purl).

2 Make the templates
Trace the templates from page 63 onto thin paper. Carefully cut them out.

Knit stitch

Fold the body over halfway down the strip.

Stockinette stitch

Instead of **stockinette** stitch, you can make me in **knit stitch**.

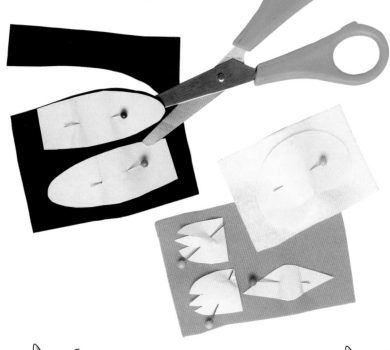

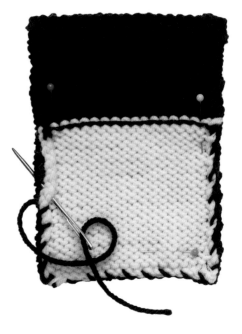

 ### 3 Cut out the felt pieces

Pin your paper templates onto felt and carefully cut out the flippers, feet, and beak.

 ### 4 Sew up the body

With right sides together, fold the body in half. Sew around the edges, leaving a gap at the side of the head for the filling. Turn the body right side out.

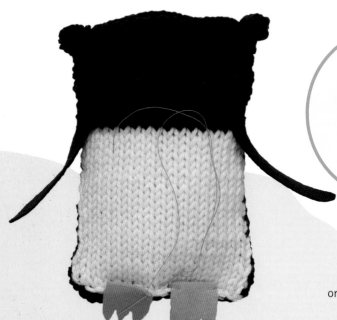

Sew the beak onto the penguin's white face.

 ### 7 Attach feet

Sew the feet onto the front of Percy's body.

8 Sew on the face

Sew around the face to hold it in place.

Now you can see the **right side** with black knit stitch and white stockinette stitch.

Sew up each corner of the head to make the ears.

Hey, wait for me!

⭐ **5** **Stuff with the filling**
Push polyfill into the body with a pencil. Sew the gap closed to hold the filling in place.

⭐ **6** **Add the flippers**
Sew a flipper onto each side of the body.

Sequins make good eyes. Beads or buttons also work well.

Glue
Use fabric glue to stick on the eyes. It's a bit sticky and tricky, so ask an adult to help you.

⭐ **9** **Add the eyes**
Use a little glue to attach the eyes.

Wheee... go with the floe!

Sally
the snake

This striped snake is a real charmer. She's made with a special variegated yarn, but you can use separate colors if you like.

Cast on 30 stitches

You will need

DK-weight variegated yarn
• pair of size 6 (4mm) knitting
needles • tapestry needle • thin
paper • polyfill • felt • buttons
• needle and thread

The variegated yarn
creates irregular
stripes that are perfect
for Sally's body.

**Variegated
yarn** works like
magic! Just keep
knitting and see how
the colors change all
by themselves.

Make Sally's body as long as you like.

1 Knit the body
Cast on 30 stitches. Keep
knitting until your knitting
is about 29in (74cm) long.

2 Make the templates
Trace the tongue and eye templates
from page 62 onto thin paper.
Carefully cut them out.

Top tip
To make a rattlesnake, put a bell inside the tail of your snake.

Jingle
Jangle

⭐ 3
Close up the tail
Sew running stitch around one short edge. Pull the yarn tight and secure with a stitch.

Stuff Sally as evenly as you

Pull the thread tight.

⭐ 6
Sew the head
Use running stitch to sew around the edge of the head. Pull the thread tight and secure with a stitch.

⭐ 7
Cut out the felt pieces
Pin your paper templates onto felt and carefully cut out two eyes and a tongue.

⭐ 8
Attach the eyes
Sew one button and felt circle onto each side of Sally's head.

★ 4 **Sew the body**
Sew up part of the body, then stuff it.
Repeat all the way up the body.

★ 5 **Stuff the head**
Finally, stuff Sally's head.

can so she looks smooth.

Sew Sally in a contrasting color of thread.

This colorful snake is made from **four colors of yarn**. He looks different—but he's just as good-looking as Sally.

★ 9 **Sew on the tongue**
Sew the forked tongue to the front of her head.

Hello, my name is Bill. I'm a banded snake.

Templates

Use these handy templates to cut out the felt shapes you'll need to make the projects in this book.

How to make a template

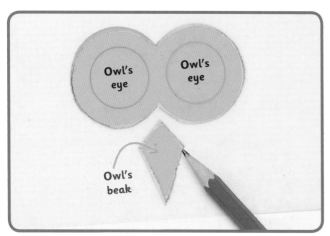

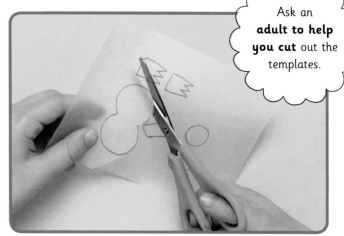

Ask an **adult to help you cut** out the templates.

1 **Draw the templates**
Place thin paper over the templates shown here. Then trace them carefully.

2 **Cut out the templates**
Cut carefully around the shapes, then follow the instructions for the project.

Bat from page 46

Bat's wings

Attach to the body along this line.

Bat's ears x 2

Snake's eyes x 2

Snake's tongue

Snake from page 58

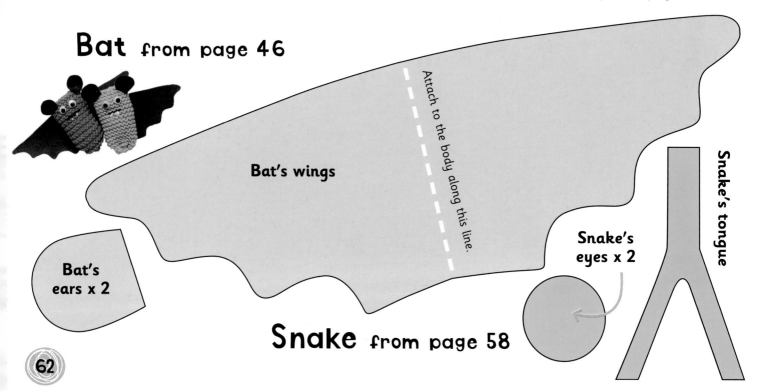

Sheep from page 34

Adult sheep's legs

Adult sheep's head

Lamb's head

Lamb's legs

Ram's horns

Owl from page 30

Owl's face

Owl's eye

Owl's eye

Owl's feet x 2

Owl's beak

Owl's wings x 2

Draw around the templates carefully.

Penguin from page 54

Penguin's face

Penguin's beak

fold

Penguin's feet x 2

Penguin's flippers x 2

63

Index

A, B, C, D

E, F, G

H, I, J, K

L, M, N,

O, P, Q

R, S, T, U

V, W, X, Y, Z

Acknowledgments

With thanks to Kathryn Meeker, Wendy Horobin and Toby Mann for proofreading.

With special thanks to model Eleanor Moore-Smith; Hannah Moore for creating the projects; and Sandra Moore for knitting and making them.

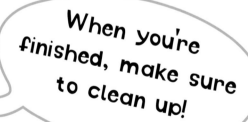

When you're finished, make sure to clean up!